SPAIN

hello friend

India office: A-81, Sector V, Noida, 201301
E-mail: hellofriend@brijbasiartpress.com

Written by: TANYA LUTHER AGARWAL

Edited by: KIRTI KAUL, EMAN CHOWDHARY

Art Director: SANJAY DHIMAN, PRIYABRATA ROY CHOWDHURY

Designed by: RAVINDER SINGH

Ilustrated by: CHANDOO, SHIJU, R. GURUNG, RAJEEV, MANOJ, VIKASH, AJAY, SUSHANTA KAR, PRINCE, RAHUL, RAJENDRA, ARIJIT CHOUDHURY AND ANEESH

ISBN: 81-8385-157-6

CONTENTS

HISTORY OF SPAIN	6-7
MONARCHY	8-9
CAPITAL CITY	10-11
MAJOR CITIES	12-13
HERITAGE CITIES-I	14-15
HERITAGE CITIES-II	16-17
LIVING IN SPAIN	18-19
FIESTA-I	20-21
FIESTA-II	22-23
FOOD	24-25
SPORTS	26-27
FAMOUS SPANIARDS-THEN	28-29
FAMOUS SPANIARDS-NOW	30-31
MUST EXPERIENCE	32-33
SUNNY SPAIN	34-35
SPAIN SAFARI-I	36-37
SPAIN SAFARI-II	38-39
SOUVENIRS OF SPAIN	40-41
FUN 'N' SPAIN	42-43
DID YOU KNOW?	44-45
KNOW YOUR SPANISH	46

HISTORY OF SPAIN

Man has inhabited Spain, or the Iberian Peninsula, since 15,000 BC. People lived in caves and hunted wild animals. They left behind wonderful paintings of these animals on the cave walls. The first invaders were the Iberians, who came from Africa. The Phoenicians from Lebanon, the Greeks, the Celts and the Carthaginians followed. After them, came the Romans, the Visigoths and the Moors. Then Christopher Columbus made some remarkable discoveries of countries around the world. This was also the time that marked the end of the Moorish reign. It was only after this that Spain began to change, grow and prosper.

Romans

It took two hundred years for the Romans to gain control of Spain after they defeated the Carthaginians. They stayed on and ruled for another four hundred years. Under the Roman rule, Spain became an extremely important cultural centre, second only to Italy. Spanish language also began to develop its own identity. Andalucia was rich in its mines and granaries and it brought great wealth at that time. The Romans had riches beyond compare, but their greed and selfishness weakened their stand against the invasion of the barbarians, the Visigoths.

The Visigoths and the Moors

In the fifth century, barbarians from Central Europe, the Visigoths, invaded Spain. They were extremely cruel and had no interest in the problems of the people, or in the working of the government. In the early 700's, the Spanish people, along with the Jews and the slaves, got together and helped the Muslim invaders, the Moors, to conquer their land. This was done in order to defeat the Visigoths. The Moors ruled the area of Andalucia for over seven hundred years, making it a centre for art, trade and culture. The Christian forces finally defeated the Moors in 1492.

Aragon and Castile

For the first time in 1479, Spain became a united country when Fernando V of Aragon and Isabella I of Castile got married. Christopher Columbus sailed the world and brought back with him riches and wealth. The Spanish army was strong and remained undefeated for 150 years. The Spanish kingdom spread out to Portugal, Italy, the Netherlands, Germany and Austria. Several rulers followed–Carlos I, Philip IV, Philip V (the first Bourbon), King Carlos IV and Fernando VII were among them. They could not hold their control over their territories and by the 1800s, the country lost almost all its power in Europe.

MONARCHY-NOW AND THEN

From 1936 to 1939, Spain went through its worst civil war. People were unhappy because inept heads were ruling the country. More than 500,000 people lost their lives. To make things worse, General Francisco Franco, a dictator, took over and led the country through terrible times for over 35 years. Before he died in 1975, he named Prince Juan Carlos of Bourbon his successor. Carlos realised the need to bring in democracy and was responsible for improving the country and the lives of the people. In 1986, Spain joined the European Union and now carries the official Euro as its currency.

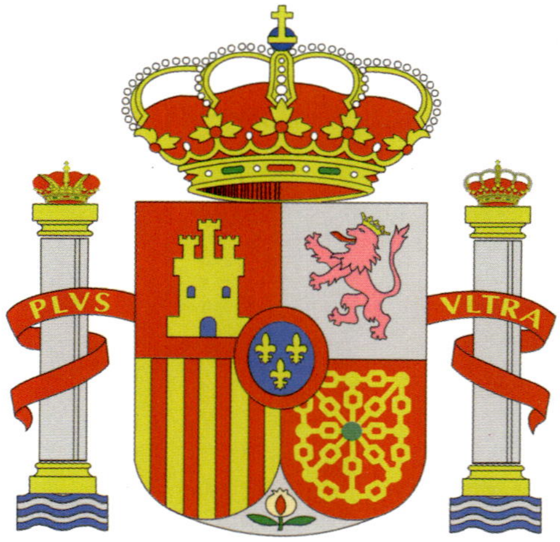

Spanish Coat of Arms

King Juan Carlos I

Spain and what it looks like

Spain occupies approximately 80%, of the Iberian Peninsula in the Southwest of Europe. The remaining 20% is occupied by Portugal. In the north, Spain borders on France and Andorra, with the Pyrenees as a natural frontier. The Balearic Islands (Mallorca, Menorca and Ibiza) in the Mediterranean Sea, Canary Islands in Atlantic Ocean, and Ceuta and Melilla located in northern Africa, also make up the Spanish territory. Spain is divided into 50 provinces, which are further grouped into 17 autonomous communities and two autonomous cities. These work independently and even have their individual flags.

Spanish Euro coin

Flag of Spain

The Spanish flag is sometimes shown without the coat of arms. It has three horizontal bands with a yellow band in the middle. The coat of arms on the flag includes the royal seal framed by the Pillars of Hercules, which represent Gibraltar and Ceuta. In 1981, this became the official flag of Spain. One legend says that the colours of the flag are picked up from the bullfight arena–red standing for the bullfighter's blood and yellow for the sand in the arena. But this is not true. The colours of the flag were actually chosen from King Ferdinand's coat of arms.The Spanish pledge to the flag is called the 'Jura de Bandera' meaning 'oath of the flag'.

The 'Coat of Arms' was actually the cloth cape or the coat that the knights wore over their armour to protect themselves from direct sunlight. This garment was often decorated with the arms, exactly as they were on the shield. The Spanish Coat of Arms is made up of six other coats of arms. The crown represents the Royal Spanish kingdom, the lion is from the Kingdom of Leon, the Pillars of Hercules are from the Kingdom of Castile, the pomegranate flower is from Granada, the red and yellow stripes belong to Aragon and the *fleur-de-lis* is from the House of Bourbon.

ANDALUCIA

ARAGON

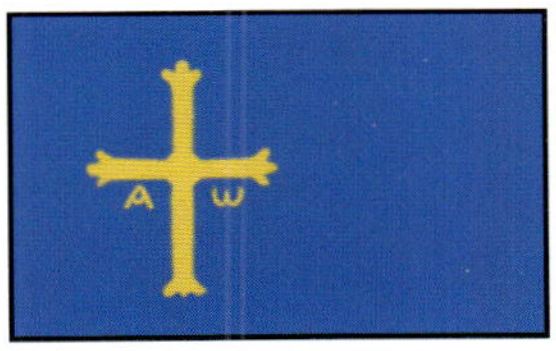

ASTURIAS

BALEARIC ISLANDS

CASTILE AND LEON

CATALUNYA

BASQUE COUNTRY

FLAG OF SPAIN

CAPITAL CITY

Madrid is the capital and the largest city of Spain, located on the Manzanares River. An interesting mix of over three million people, or 'madrilenos', inhabit Madrid, making it an exciting and a vivacious city. It is also the most popular tourist destination in Spain. Madrid offers not just amazing places to see, but also has a friendly and welcoming air to it. Madrid has a Mediterranean climate with fresh winters and warm summers. Spring (March through May) and October are the best times to be in Madrid. The most important cultural spot in Madrid is the 'Golden Triangle of Art' on Paseo del Prado. Located here are three of the world's most famous museums. The other great places to see here are the Gran Via, the Metropolis Building, the El Retiro park and the Temple Debod.

Prado Museum

Prado Museum (Museo del Prado)

The museum building was constructed in the 18th century during the reign of Charles III. At one point in time, it was even used as a cavalry and gunpowder store for Napoleon's troops. 'Prado' in Spanish means meadow, and this grand building stands in the Paseo del Prado area. This museum carries 8,600 paintings of world famous artistes like Goya, Velazquez, Botticelli, Rembrandt, Raphael etc. and other prized paintings and sculptures from the 14th to the 19th century.

Plazas

Although a plaza means a square, in Madrid they come in different shapes–oval, rectangular, square or round. They are central places, where local people come together, especially for celebrations. The Plaza de la Cibeles is located at one of the busiest road crossings in the city.

Fountain of Goddess Cibeles

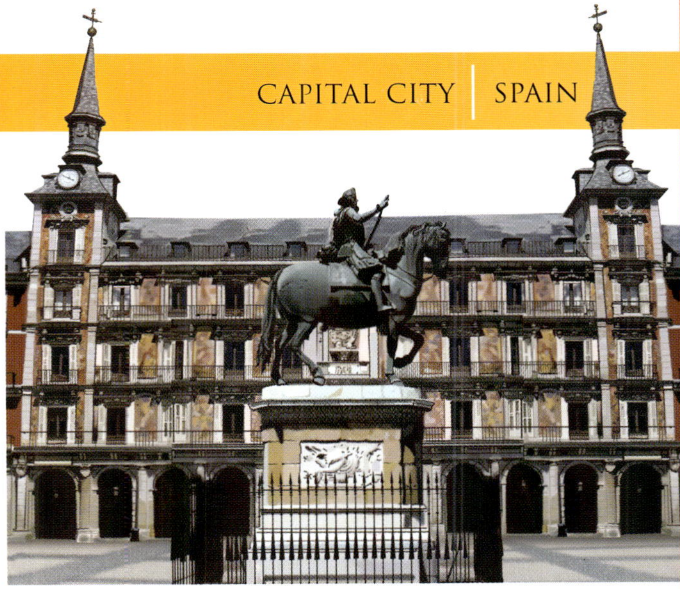

▲ *Plaza Mayor*

Plaza Mayor

This 17th century plaza has been the site of executions, weddings, bullfights and inquistion trials. These days tourists can enjoy a free concert, take a stroll, or browse through the coin and stamp collections on Sundays.

▲ *Sculpture of a bear eating the fruit of Madroño*

Puerta del Sol

The Puerta del Sol is one of the most well-known and busiest places in Spain. This is also the centre of the 'zero kilometre' or the offical starting point of six of Spain's main highways. In the 15th century, the Puerta del Sol was one of the gates in the city wall that surrounded Madrid.
A statue of Charles III stands in the square along with a bronze sculpture of a bear eating the fruit of the Madron tree (a cousin of the strawberry fruit). The name Madrid, in fact, comes from the word Madroño.

Palacio Real de Madrid

The Palacio Real de Madrid is the official residence of the King of Spain. Although King Juan Carlos and his family do not live in it, the Palace is used for state occasions.

The Palace of Madrid ▼

MAJOR CITIES

Barcelona

Barcelona, the capital of Catalonia, is the second largest city in Spain, both in size and in population. It is a charming city that has a good mix of the historic and the modern–buildings, towns, beaches etc. In 1992, Barcelona became the host for the Olympic games. *Las Ramblas,* a lively street, leads to the harbour and the Mediterranean Sea. Other interesting places are The Maritime Museum, the Temple Expiatori de la Sagrada Familia, the Picasso Museum, and the Monsterrat Monastery. Central Barcelona has so many amazing sites that it would take many days to see them all.

Barcelona harbour

Valencia

Valencia, also known as the land of flowers, is the third largest city in Spain and lies along the Costa Brava Coast. The Torres de Serrano and the Torres de Quart are the two gates that remain of the original walls of the city. The tower, Torres de Quart, built in 1994, is an interesting sight, as one can still see the walls that were damaged from shelling during the war of independence against the French. The beautiful Plaza de la Virgen, a Roman square, was built using many different architectural styles.

Plaza de la Virgen

Torres de Quart, Valencia

Seville

On the banks of the Guadalquivir River is the largest city of Southern Spain, Seville. It is the capital of Andalucia and the province Sevilla. This is the land of the traditional Spanish dance, the flamenco, and has the most unique Easter celebrations that last over two weeks. The La Giralda Cathedral of Seville is the largest of all medieval and gothic cathedrals in the world. Binoculars in hand, the top of the Torre de Oro, a tower, offers a spectacular view of the Guadalaquivir river. From there, it wouldn't be hard to imagine a river full of sailing ships hollering 'Ships ahoy'! The 'Giralda Tower' was originally a 'minaret',and part of the Moorish mosque, that preceded the cathedral. In 1248, the minaret was considered a marvel even by Fernando III, who made sure that the tower was protected before he conquered the city of Seville.

La Giralda Cathedral, Seville

WORLD HERITAGE CITIES-I

UNESCO (United Nations Educational Scientific and Cultural Organisation) strives to look after, and protect the culture and the history of cities around the world. It has set up an organisation, which chooses traditional cities and gives them the title of 'World Heritage City'. By doing this, it helps and protects a city, so that it is able to maintain its beauty and culture. Spain is the only country in the world that has eight World Heritage Cities.

Entrance to the city of Toledo

Toledo

Toledo, capital of Castile-La Mancha, sits pretty on a hill above the Tagus River. This city is over 18 centuries old. If a visitor is looking for monuments, he need not look any further. Toledo is one of the Spanish cities, which has several monuments. It is also known as the 'city of three cultures' as the Christians, Arabs and the Jews lived here together for centuries. With churches, synagogues, palaces, fortresses and mosques built in different styles, Toledo looks like an open-air museum. Toledo was, and still is, best known for its swords.

Avila de los Caballeros (Avila of the Knights)

Avila, the city of saints and knights, is surrounded by the Sierra de Gredos mountains. It is the capital of Castile-Leon. The city walls were built in the 11th century and they still stand around the city, looking majestic. The walls are about 9 feet wide and 36 feet high with 82 large towers and nine gates. Within the city, are some beautiful churches and religious buildings. One look at them, and it becomes easy to understand why is it a Heritage City.

City wall of Avila

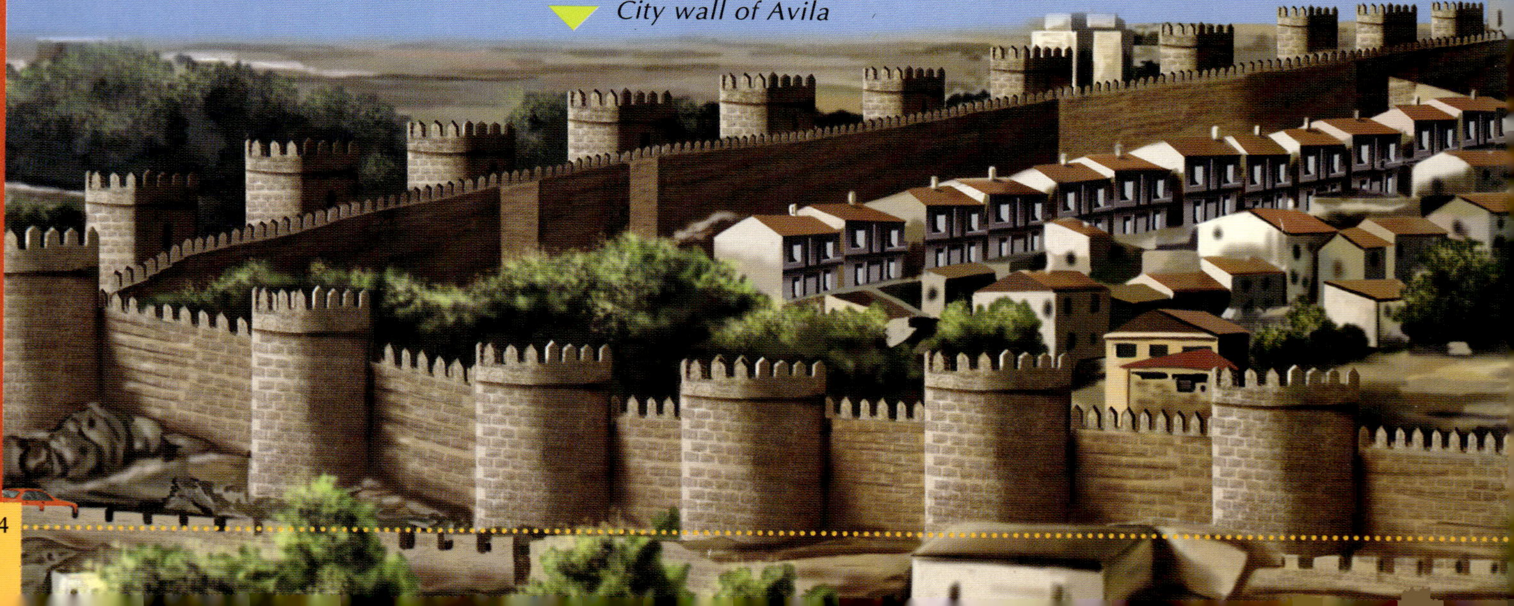

Salamanca

The Iberians built Salamanca in pre-historic times. The Romans ruled Salamanca and a bridge constructed then, still stands over the Tormes river. Even today, it is intact with 15 of its original arches. In the 13th century, King Alfonso IX of Leon built the world famous University of Salamanca here. Felipe V built the Plaza Mayor, the largest plaza in Spain. Two cathedrals, 'La Catedral Vieja' and 'La Catedral Nueva', built about three centuries apart, in two different architectural styles, are the most outstanding sights in Salamanca.

Cathedral, Santiago

Santiago de Compostela

Santiago de Compostela is the capital of Galicia and lies between the Galician rivers, Tambre and Ulla. Today, it looks modern but has its traditional buildings standing side by side. Legend has it that the beginnings of this city go back to a time, when a bishop informed King Alfonso II of the miraculous discovery of a tomb with the body of Santiago, St. James the Apostle. The most prominent monument here is the Cathedral built by King Alfonso II.

Old and new Cathedrals, Salamanca

WORLD HERITAGE CITIES-II

Mosque Cathedral, Cordoba

Segovia

Segovia rests on high ground between the channels of the rivers, Eresma and Clamores. It has three fabulous monuments–the Roman Aqueduct, built around 50 AD, a Cathedral from the 16th century and the Royal fortress-castle built in the 15th century. The Aqueduct was built to channel water from the river Frio. The castle-fortress was built on sheer cliffs and it can easily be called the 'most photographed' castle in Spain. A military museum can be found inside it, and taking the spiral steps up to the top of the castle, gives a stunning view of the city.

Cordoba

Cordoba, an ancient city, was built to navigate the Guadalquivir river. It was once the capital of Hispania Ulterior under the Roman Empire as well as the capital of the Umayyad Caliphate. Both Roman and Muslim influences can be seen in its architecture. The Mezquita, great mosque of Cordoba, is the best example of the beautiful mix of styles and religions. Started in the 8th century and completed only in the 10th century, the mosque has exquisite arches that support the roofs. In the 16th century, a cathedral was built inside the mosque!

Although a modern city today, Cordoba continues to blend the old-world charm with the new.

Roman Aqueduct, Segovia

Cuenca

Cuenca is also known as the 'Eagles' Nest' because it rests high on a hill. The city is separated from the rivers, Jucar and Huecar, by deep ravines. Cuenca is a small city built on rocks. The space on the rocks being limited, many houses are partly hanging over the cliff. Thanks to natural erosion, the rocks here resemble elephants, crocodiles, landscapes and so on.

Hanging houses, Cuenca

Caceres

Caceres too, like Cuenca, lies on a hill. The Romans, the Arabs and then the Christians ruled it. It became a city of great wealth, which led to the building of lavish homes and palaces. To show their wealth, people constructed watchtowers that led to squabbles amongst families. Therefore, Queen Isabella ordered all but one, the Torre de la Ciguena, to be destroyed.

Torre de la Ciguena

LIVING IN SPAIN

Spanish homes or 'pueblos blancos', were built to cope with the sometimes harsh Mediterranean climate. The original whitewashed village houses were designed to reflect the hot Spanish Sun. They were also built with small windows to keep the cool air in and the heat out. Old Ibizan houses had small rooms and thick external walls. Basements in these houses were built to keep animals or to store wine. Even today, they remain charming and full of character. 'Pallozas' were round or oval houses built on hill slopes. They had stone walls and thatched roofs.

Old Ibizan houses

Spanish Attire

In the past, various regions of Spain had their own distinct regional dress. These days, however, most people in Spain dress like their counterparts in any other European country. The Spanish love to put on their traditional clothes for the fiestas. While the men wear wide sombreros and flowing white shirts, the women wear brightly coloured dresses. In Spain, the people of Barcelona are perhaps the most stylish. Madrid's national dress is called the 'Chulapo' or 'Chulapa'.

Traditional Spanish scarf, hat and comb

Palloza

Spanish People and Families

Just like the climate and the landscape of Spain, the people of this land are warm and inviting to friends and guests alike. The Spaniards are fun loving people. They know how to enjoy life and love eating and partying. A patriotic nation of people, they are just as fiercely loyal to their families. In traditional Spain, children continue to remain very closely connected with their families, well into their adulthood. Traditional families in Spain often have three generations living together. It is not uncommon for sons and daughters to live with their parents, until they get married. Every Spaniard, whether male or female, has three names–a g ven name (nombre) and two surnames or family names (apellidos).

A modern Spanish house

FIESTA-I

La Tomatina

A fiesta is a celebration or a festivity. In Spain, fiestas are colourful, exciting and noisy but always a lot of fun. People make merry on the streets with processions, marching bands and even fireworks! Fiestas could be religious, ceremonial or otherwise. Some are local events in a village, while others have the entire nation celebrating it. The Spanish have a fiesta marked on their calendar, every day of the year. No matter which time of the year you go to Spain, you can be sure that you will get to join in the fun of a fiesta.

La Tomatina

This is the world's biggest, soggiest and the messiest tomato fight, held in the village of Bunol. Thousands of people fling truckloads of red juicy tomatoes on one another. The rule is simple–tomatoes and only tomatoes can be pelted, at anyone who is sitting, standing, lying, moving, not moving, bending, and not bending... Did someone say you couldn't have fun when you grew up?

San Fermin Festival, Pamplona

San Fermin Festival

On July 7 every year, you can, along with hundreds of others, tie a red bandana around your neck and run down the narrow streets of Pamplona with ten bulls chasing you. Why? Just for fun, of course. San Fermin is the patron saint of Navarra, and bulls are a part of the old Spanish tradition. The fiesta lasts a week, with dare devils running as madly as the bulls.

Las Fallas Festival-The Fires

From the 13th to the 18th of March, the streets of Valencia buzz with energy and gaiety. Enormous figures and models, made from paper-mache, tower the 350 intersections of the city. The Valencians take a whole year to build the mighty effigies. These are stuffed with firecrackers and burnt after a whole week of partying on the streets. The ninots or models are life-like and some are several storeys tall.
One prize-winning ninot is spared from destruction and it gets exhibited until the following year. A pyrotechnic show at midnight can leave you wide-eyed and mouth open!

A festive couple

The Water Festival

If you feel lazy to take a shower, step out on the streets of Vilagarcia de Arousa on August 16, and let the crowds clean you. On the hottest day of the year, the party-goers use everything from hosepipes, water hydrants to buckets and even water-filled balloons to drench one another. If the enthusiasm looks like it is about to die out, the drum beats are sure to get the crowds excited. And if the water seems like it is running out, fire engines are called in to save the party. You are sure to yell-'soaking wet'!

The festival of San Juan

This festival is celebrated all over Spain. On June 23, the shortest night of the year in the Northern Hemisphere, the Spaniards find one more reason to celebrate with bonfires, fireworks, music and dancing. They believe that burning bonfires on this night can cure people of skin diseases and purify the body and the soul. You will actually be encouraged to jump over a bonfire three times, to fix any bad events taking place in your life. In Ciutadella, you can throw sackfull of hazelnuts at people you love. Parents beware!

San Juan Festival

San Isidro

The patron saint of farmers, San Isidro, was a poor but generous, and a popular farmer. To honour him, the Plaza Mayor in Madrid turns into a huge party place for nine days. The celebrations start from the 15th of May. People make a pilgrimage to the saint's meadow and drink the holy water from his fountain. The merry-making has people dressed traditionally in 'Chulapo'. There is the all-time favourite snack 'Barquillos', a bread that is dipped in chocolate. Music and dance is part of the celebrations but the biggest attraction is the ultimate bullfighting show.

Saint San Isidro

La Tamborrada

If you are always being told to keep your voice down, San Sebastian is the place to be at, on the 19th and the 20th of January. For a whole day and night, the otherwise sleepy town roars with sounds of drums and barrels being beaten by immaculately uniformed marchers. Although a short festival, the locals party almost non-stop for 24 hours to honour their saint Donostia of San Sebastian in an almost deafening din.

La Tamborrada

Carnivals in Tenerife

For all those who love fancy dress shows, and love to continue dressing up for 27 days, join the Spaniards in Tenerife in the month of January. As with all Spanish fiestas, there is gaiety, music and dance, and unlimited fun to be had. There are street processions, dance and music competitions and a carnival Queen is also chosen. There is colour on the streets, in costumes and of course, in the smiles of all who join in!

During the summer fiestas in Madrid, people drink 'limonada' made up of wine, 7up, lemons and peaches.

Carnival in Tenerife

FOOD

The beauty of Spanish food is not in just how colourful it looks, but also in the fact that it has been influenced by the different cultures that it was ruled by–the Romans, Visigoths, Moors, Phoenicians, Greeks and the Arabs. The Romans influenced Spanish cooking when they developed wine, oil and wheat production. The Moors introduced olives, oranges, lemons, aubergines and rice. On their discovery of the Americas, the Spanish brought back with them, potatoes, maize, cocoa and pepper.

A Typical Day of Spanish Food

Breakfast : Desayuno
Bollos (rolls with jam)
White coffee or thick hot chocolate
Con Churros (sweet, fried batter)
Lunch/La Comida : 3-course meal
Starters-salad, vegetables, lentil stew, and omelette
Soup
Main course-fish and/or meat, lamb, fried food
Dinner/La Cena : 3-course meal as above.

Lunch is the biggest meal of the day running late into the afternoon. Dinner begins well after 9 at night and carries through to midnight.

Spanish Olives

Paella being prepared

Paella

Paella, (pie-a-yah), is a colourful blend of rice, shrimp, chicken, tomato, chorizo, sausage, mussels, and saffron! Even today, it is prepared as the 19th century Valencian field labourers did–in a flat pan cooked over open fires! In earlier days, farmhands used rice, and threw in any available edibles like snails, vegetables and artichokes. All over Spain, paella is consumed with all kinds of variations. It is cheap, full of flavour, and very filling. When in Spain, the paella has to be tried, tasted and relished.

Tapas

If you don't speak Spanish but can say 'tapas', you will surely find a place to eat! Every Spaniard has a favourite 'tasca' or a tapas bar, where they meet up with friends, relatives or business acquaintances. Tapas are mini snacks. They could be made with cheese, fish, eggs, dips, savoury pastries, squids, prawns, meatballs, anchovies etc. Every region of Spain has its own version of the tapas. With so much variety, would you be able to try them all?

Tapas

Cheese

As with the food, Spanish cheese also comes in many different forms. 'Cabrales' is a spicy cheese from Asturias and made from cow milk. The Basque Country makes a popular 'Idiazabal' from sheep milk. It has a sharp flavour and is surprisingly chewy. However, a favourite with the children is the soft and creamy 'Galician Tetilla' from the provinces of Pontevedra and Lugo. But the king of Spanish cheese is undoubtedly the 'Manchego.' It is cylindrical in shape, creamy, nutty and salty-spicy in taste. Look for the zig-zag imprint on this cheese.

Spanish Cheese

SPORTS IN SPAIN

The Spanish people simply love sports. With the Sun shining on their land, almost all through the year, it is not surprising to know that they seek the outdoors and all kinds of sports. The natural landscape in Spain makes it possible for many different kinds of sports to be enjoyed. Being the second most mountainous country in Europe, with the 'Pyrenees' and the 'Picos de Europa' peaks as high as 8600 feet, mountaineering, rock climbing, hiking and trekking are very popular. The rivers and streams of these mountains are ideal for freshwater fishing. Swimming, water-skiing and windsurfing are also sports to be enjoyed. In Tarifa, on the Straits of Gibraltar, windsurfing world championships are held. Sailing, along the 4000-km coastline too, is a favourite as well.

Playing Soccer

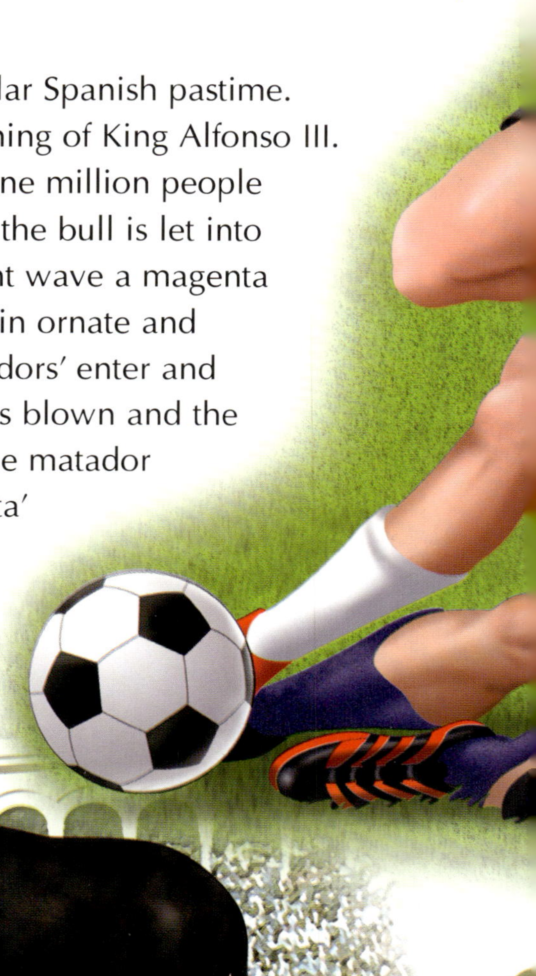

Bullfighting

Watching a bullfight, known as a 'corrida', is the most popular Spanish pastime. The first bullfight was held in 711 AD to celebrate the crowning of King Alfonso III. Today, there are 70 bullrings in Andalucia alone, and over one million people watch bullfights every year. This is how a bull is fought–first the bull is let into the ring, then the bullfighter or the 'matador' and his assistant wave a magenta cape in front of the bull to make it charge. Both are dressed in ornate and colourful costumes. A trumpet is blown; fighters called 'picadors' enter and weaken the bull by piercing spears into it. Another trumpet is blown and the matador begins the 'faena', his artful dance with the bull. The matador holds a thick crimson cloth draped over a stick called 'muleta' and sways it dramatically to the cheers of 'Ole' from the excited audience.

Matador fighting a bull

Soccer

In Spain, soccer is the 'king of sports'. It was first played in the Spanish mines by the Scottish and the English workers, way back in 1873. Most soccer games are played on Sundays from September to May. Two of the most famous Spanish League club teams are 'Real Madrid' and 'F C Barcelona' and they meet in the stadium to play the most pulsating match called the 'El Derby'. The game has a turnout of more than 100,000 fans. Then, there is the Spanish national football team that plays international matches like the World Cup soccer. The Spanish team has qualified for the World Cup at least nine times. The team's t-shirt is an outstanding red coloured one.

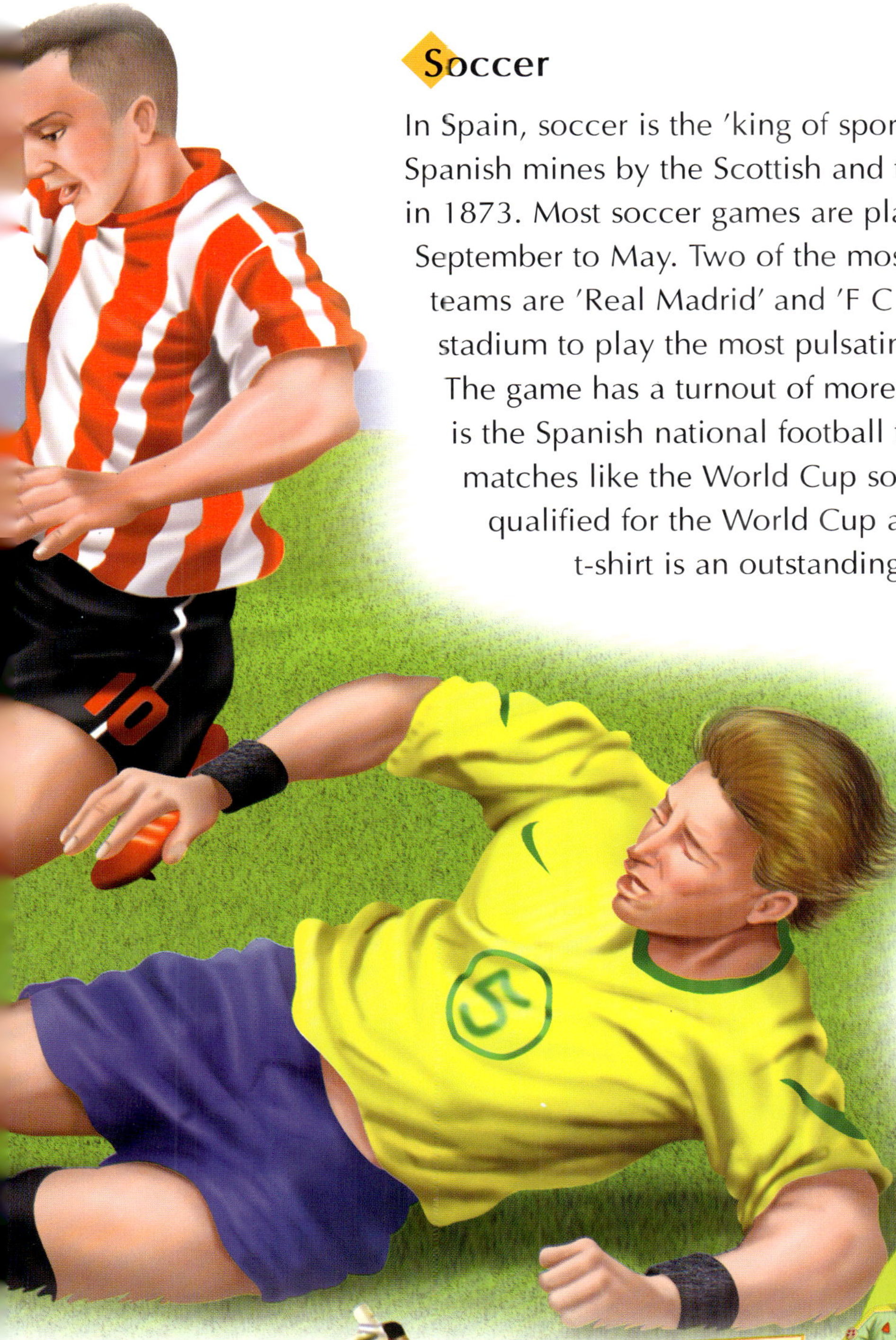

FC Bercelona jersey

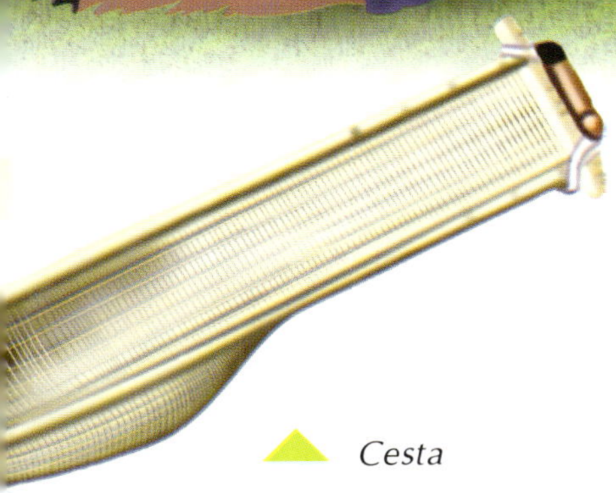

Cesta

FAMOUS SPANIARDS-THEN

Self-portrait, Pablo Picasso

The golden age of Spanish exploration and conquest is important, not just historically but also because of the notable personalities that became immortal. Spain gave to the world, talented artists, successful explorers, and brilliant scientists. Ferdinand and Queen Isabella of the 15th century were great rulers. Christopher Columbus, was perhaps the greatest Spanish explorer, who discovered native America. Between the 16th and the 18th century, Spanish art, architecture, music, and literature flourished with great names like El Greco, Valazquez, Goya, Picasso, Dali, Juan Boscan, Luis de Gongora and Villegas. Manuel de Falla was a brilliant music composer. Santiago Cajal was the first Nobel Prize winner for medicine. Jaime Ferran discovered the vaccine for cholera. These Spaniards took their nation to great heights.

Diego Valazquez (1599-1660)

Valazquez can easily be called one of Spain's greatest painters. Born in a noble family in Seville, Valasquez learned painting from a teacher and also by observing nature. He moved to Madrid at the age of 19, and at 24, he painted a portrait of Philip IV. He became a court painter and went on to paint everyday subjects, still life, portraits, religious scenes, and landscapes. He used colour, light, space and strokes in such a brilliant manner that his paintings seemed to be alive and breathing. The horses, he painted, looked like they would step out of the canvas to ride away. The clothes he painted on the royalty-lace, silk and net, appear so real that one can easily identify the fabric. His painting 'Las Meninas' was painted as a photograph, long before the camera was invented.

Diego Valazquez

Antoni Gaudí (1852-1926)

The son of a coppersmith, Gaudi went on to become one of Spain's most celebrated architects. What makes his architectural style unique is that his designs used curves in stone and concrete effortlessly. This made the buildings look different. Gaudi was fascinated by nature. He imitated the way trees and humans grow and stand upright. Most of his designs had features taken from nature.

Antoni Gaudi

Cervantes

Miguel de Cervantes (1547-1616)

Cervantes is known as one of the greatest Spanish writers. He was a poet, playwright and a novelist. Cervantes wrote the first modern novel and one of the greatest works in literature, Don Quixote. The main character of the novel is an elderly knight, who sets out on his old horse, Rosinante, to seek adventure. The story has been translated into several languages. It has also been made into plays, ballets, operas, films and musicals. The book has also inspired music composers like Strauss and Falla.

FAMOUS SPANIARDS-NOW

Writer Arturo Perez Reverte

Spain has produced notable personalities in the fields of science, art, literature, business, politics and entertainment. Fermin Cacho Ruiz (an Olympic gold medallist in atheletics), Javier Castillejo (a world champion boxer), and Alfredo Di Stefano (soccer) are some world-class sports personalities. Ferran Adrià Acosta is considered one of the best chefs in the world. Teresa Berganza is a well-known Spanish opera singer and Pedro Francisco Duque is an astronaut and a veteran of two space missions. Teresa Barbero, Ramon Nieto and Francisco Umbral are some famous Spanish writers. Arturo Perez Reverte, journalist and best-selling novelist, deserves a special mention. In a country where reading is not a popular pastime, Reverte is one of Spain's most translated writers.

The Iglesias Legacy

Julio Iglesias is one of the best selling Spanish singers of all times. He has sold over 250,000,000 records in different languages and has performed in about 5,000 concerts during his career. He was a professional soccer player with Real Madrid until an accident left him bed-ridden for a while. While recuperating, he began to write songs. This was the beginning of a new career for Iglesias. He won several Grammy awards and topped the Billboard charts for many years. His son, Enrique, went on to follow his footsteps. Enrique let his father know about his ambition only after he signed his first record deal. The record sold more than a million copies in its first three months! Within three years, Iglesias Jr. went on to become the biggest selling Spanish artist in the world.

Julio Iglesias

Actor Antonio Banderas

Antonio Banderas

Handsome, charming and multi-talented Antonio Banderas has starred in over 50 films. The Hollywood film, 'The Mask of Zorro', made this Spanish actor an international star.

Miguel Indurain

This Spaniard began cycling for fun. Today, he remains the only cyclist to have won five consecutive Tour de France races. He rode a bicycle for the first time at the age of nine!

Miguel Indurain

Penelope Cruz

Elegant and graceful, Madrid born Penelope Cruz has starred in several films including the Oscar-winning, 'Belle Epoque'.

Actress Penelope Cruz

Cristina Sánchez de Pablos

The first woman bullfighter in modern times, Cristina Sánchez de Pablos, has enjoyed local as well as international fame. A week afer she turned 21, Cristina debuted as a bullfighter in Madrid. During her career of six years, she cut a total of 316 bull ears at the bullrings of Spain, Ecuador and Mexico.

Cristina Sanchez

MUST EXPERIENCE

If you have wondered what a palaeontologist does, and the sound of the word dinosaur gets you excited, then make sure you plan on being in La Rioja, Asturias, Teruel or Soria. Spain is an international point of reference in palaeontology because the ichnites or fossil footprints of dinosaurs found here, are considered amongst the world's most important for their quality and variety. In Conargo, one can see tracks of such amazing quality that it seems as if the dinosaurs recently passed by. The largest tracks in the whole world are found in Ribadesella in Asturias. So, put on your hat and outdoor gear, and set out with a magnifying glass on well-marked trails on a journey back in time.

Go Wild

About 32 kilometres east of Madrid is the Safari Park of Madrid, where wild animals live in their natural habitat. Visitors can drive through the park and see a huge expanse with nearly 500 animals, ranging from lazing tigers, monkeys and giraffes to elephants and hippos bathing in the lakes. You can feed wild boars and dwarf goats or ride a pony or a camel.

The Flooded Forest

Looking for a dinosaur fossil

The Spiral Staircase, Cosmo Caixa

The Cosmo Caixa Experience

This new and modern science museum in Barcelona is the finest in Europe. Built mostly underground, it goes down as deep as five storeys. A spiral staircase leads down to the various exhibits. The centrepiece is a massive tree trunk suspended in mid air by steel cables. There is the planetarium and the geological wall amongst other attractions. However, the most outstanding and spectacular area is the Flooded Forest, an exact reproduction of the Amazon jungle.

Go West

If cowboy hats, breeches, horses and a drawling southern American accent is your favourite pretend play, then don't miss a trip to the village of Tabernas, 26 km from Almeria city. Set in a barren landscape of canyons and rocky wasteland, this is the place where action-packed 'Westerns' like the 'The Good, The Bad and The Ugly', 'A Fistful of Dollars' and 'The Magnificent Seven' were shot. The original movie sets have been retained, and have become a tourist attraction theme park. Complete with an authentic saloon and stage coaches raising the dust, fans can enjoy a day out in Europe's only desert region. There is also a simulation of a wild west style bank robbery and staged gunfights to be watched.

A film set at Tabernas

SUNNY SPAIN

Spain has almost 4,000 kilometres of Sun and sand outlining it's map and nearly three hundred days of sunshine every year. It is no wonder then that the beaches of Spain are a favourite destination for tourists from all over the world. All this in one country and that too without the hurricanes, twisters or the typhoons! On the eastern and the southern coasts of Spain, one can dive into the Mediterranean waters. Along the west and the south, there is the Atlantic Ocean to swim in and to the north, there is the Bay of Biscay.

The Canary Islands

The seven Canary Islands are the Gran Canaria, Tenerife, Lanzarote, La Palma, La Gomera, El Hierro and Fuerteventura. Together they form an archipelago in the Atlantic Ocean. These islands are warmed by the Gulf Stream and cooled by the Atlantic breezes. The climate varies from mild and wet to warm and dry, depending on their distance from Africa and the trade winds that blow on them. They are so close to the Sahara Desert in Africa that many of their beaches were formed by sand that blew over from the desert. The Canary coast has excellent conditions for water sports such as sailing, water-skiing, kayaking and surfing. But it is windsurfing, which attracts tourists to the islands all through the year. El Médano on Tenerife, Jandía on Fuerteventura and Pozo Izquierdo on Gran Canaria are the venues for the world windsurfing championship. The archipelago's ocean depths were formed by volcanic eruptions. The mysterious underground water caves, cliffs and crevices are found nowhere else in the world and can be explored while snorkelling and scuba diving.

Canary coastline

Costa Brava

The Costa Brava coast is chiselled and shaped by the Mediterranean Sea with spectacular beaches, rugged cliffs, scenic creeks, and hidden coves. Sitting back on a 'pedalos', a two seater foot-driven boat, is a wonderful way to enjoy the waters. Swimming and snorkelling are especially fun because the waters are very clear.

Costa Brava beach

The Balearic Islands

This wonderful group of islands is divided into Gimnesias (Mallorca, Menorca and Cabrera) in the North, and Pitiusas (Ibiza y Formentera) in the Southwest. The year round excellent climate and superb beaches make this region an exciting holiday destination. Each island has its unique character and natural beauty that is different from the other. The islands of Ibiza and Minorca offer stunning beaches and coves, sparkling blue waters that are ideal for swimming in and brilliant sunshine. Ibiza has a 210 km long coastline with white sandy beaches one after another. Sailing, scuba diving, sea kayaking, and water-skiing are great ways to admire the natural beauty of this island.

Balearic Islands coastline

SPAIN SAFARI-I

Pyrenees Mountains

With nine national parks and hundreds of wildlife reserves, Spain is known to have the most beautiful, natural places in Europe. The Pyrenees Mountains are home to alpine lakes, glaciers, national reserves and game parks. Galicia, Asturias and Cantabrias, along with Basque Country, make up 'green Spain', a wet area producing a wide range of leafy, woodland vegetation. This area stretches for more than 2,000 km with cliffs, mountains, forests, rivers, beaches, deep gorges and valleys. Here purple herons, storks, ducks, brown bears, roe deer, wild boars and short-toed eagles can be found amongst the beech and oak trees. Guided bird watching is also offered in many of these forests. Along the Mediterranean Coast and further south; vineyards, almond and olive groves, and orchards of oranges and lemons can be seen. The Canary Islands in contrast, are densely forested with high volcanoes as well as barren deserts.

Safari Parks

One can watch animals in their natural habitat in nature parks like Faunia in Madrid, and Selwo on the Costa del Sol. At the Safari Park in Aldea del Fresno, located an hour from Madrid, one can travel with elephants, rhinoceros, giraffes, hippopotamus, and many other animal species. At some parks, children are taught to identify different plant species, and discover the hiding places and behaviour of squirrels, griffon vultures, roe deer and other animals.

Selwo, Costa del Sol

Vías Verdes

When 1500 km of railway tracks became useless after the trains stopped chugging on them, they were cleverly reused. These tracks offered an enjoyable and an environment friendly way of seeing the Spanish countryside. Vías Verdes means 'green ways' which basically are old, disused railway lines that have been converted into cycling and walking routes. Nature lovers, young and old, and even disabled find the Vias Verde an easy and accessible option to explore Spain. From north to south and east to west, there are 50 routes to choose from and these cover nearly thousands of kilometres.

Vias Verdes

TIEDE NATIONAL PARK

From around the landscape of the Tiede National Park in Tenerife, Canary Islands, rises the biggest volcano in Spain, Mt Tiede. Although the volcano is currently dormant, it may erupt in the future. For the fearless, a hot air balloon ride is probably the best way to see this mountain and the rest of the island. There is also a cable car ride that goes most of the way to the summit. One can see emissions of hot sulphur dioxide and other gases from here.

Mount Tiede, Canary Islands

SPAIN SAFARI-II

Ordesa National Park

The Ordesa National Park is amongst the top three in Spain. It sprawls over 56,000 acres of lush valleys and meadows and steep limestone slopes. Since the mountains here run east to west, the valley gets lots of cool moist air from the Atlantic, making it rich with plant life. With the valley ending, a glacial circle called the Circa Soasa starts. Many seasonal wildflowers such as edelweiss, entians, orchids, violets, belladonna and anemones abound this area, with stunning butterflies in the hay meadows. An amazing variety of song birds, golden eagles, Egyptian vultures, falcons and eagle owls are also found here. The Park was set up specifically to protect the ibex (wild goat) and the lammergeier, a kind of bearded vulture. So look out for them! Hiking, climbing, trekking and ambling are perhaps the best ways to explore the breathtaking sceneries. Most visitors land in the charming village of Torla and follow the trails. Another popular walk is the Circa Soasa, which takes between five to eight hours and offers a lot of beauty.

Flora and Fauna

The flora in Spain has a typical Mediterranean character. The most common trees found here are the oak, chestnut, birch, beech, and coniferous woods. The fauna has the feral cat, lynx, red deer, chameleon, mongoose, the Spanish ibex, and chamois among other mammals. One of the most striking species is the blue magpie bird found in central and southern Spain.

Ordesa National Park

Basque Country

The Basque Country in northern Spain is abundant with green landscapes and salt-water. This makes the area one of the best conserved ecological areas in Europe. It can be explored on horseback or by foot.

Basque Country

Sea Safari

Choose a calm, sunny day to step into the cool, blue waters in the Cadiz Province or the Canary Islands to watch the whales and the dolphins. Hop on a boat and spot these mammals in their natural habitat. On board, along with the guides and instructors, you can relax on the deck with drinks and food. You could also slip into the underwater viewing cabins from where the sea looks like a giant aquarium!

Canary Islands

SOUVENIRS OF SPAIN

If you are visiting Spain, the traditional Spanish gear–a poncho, Cordoba hat or sombrero, a Spanish guitar, and a bright, loud 'fallas' (festive outfit), must be bought. On your return from your vacation, you could actualy recreate a fiesta at home! Then there are leather goods, clothing, embroidery, lace, gold and silver jewellery, wickerwork, blown glass, ceramics and pottery that visitors can find just about anywhere in Spain. However, most regions have their specialities that have been produced there for generations.

In Salamanca, one can find the famed Spanish style riding boot or 'Boto' and the 'Béjar' cape. Glazed pottery from Granada is traditionally known by the name of 'Fajalauza', the place where many potters are settled. Moorish influence can be seen in the blue and the green glaze of the pottery. Guitars and castanets of the highest quality can also be found here. Alicante is known for high quality footwear. The Canaries are famous for exquisite embroidery and fine thread work as well as wickerwork. Mallorcan pearls are world famous, but the one must-buy gift for friends is the 'siurell'. Made since the time of the Arabs, siurells are clay whistles that come in all shapes and sizes–the most popular design being a man on a horseback painted white in flashes of red and green.

Siurell

Ceramic Tile

Ceramic bowl

Lladro porcelain

Three brothers of the Lladro farming family built an oven in the courtyard of their parents' house and began making small useful objects like vases and jugs. In time, their business began to flourish and sculptors and designers joined their small company. Soon, Lladro creations in porcelain began to be exported around the world. From a simple sketch, a clay model is made, which is then transformed into a mould. This mould is then filled with a secret blend of porcelain-filled liquid. Sometimes, over one hundred moulds are needed to create a single Lladro piece!

Lladro figurine

Ceramic Jug

FUN 'N' SPAIN

What good is a vacation without glee-filled screaming and a racing heartbeat? If you dare to face your fears or simply want to indulge in fun that will keep you smiling all day, then head for the best amusement and water parks in Spain.

Amusement & Theme Parks

An hour's drive south of Barcelona leads to Port Aventura theme park. The park has a recreated Mediterranean port, the Wild West, China, Polynesia and Mexico, and colonial Spain with roller coasters and other rides on the same theme. The biggest theme park in Spain is the Terra Mitica Park in Benidorm, Alicante. Here, one is swept back to the Mediterranean world of mythical civilisations. These dark and spooky rides were the first of their kind in Europe.The Isla Magica Park in Seville offers thrilling adventure with superb rides and legendary characters. The Warner Brothers Movie World in Madrid has shows, heart-thumping rides, and street pageantry.

Warner Brothers Movie World

Dragon Khan, Port Aventura

Water Parks

For all the water babies, who never grew up, there are plenty of places to drench yourself in. 50 kilometres from Marbella is Aquapark Torremolinos. This is the largest water park in Europe, spread over 70,000 square metres. There is something for everybody–hair raising rides like the kamikaze twister, vertical rides, a waves swimming pool, rides for tiny tots and even a Jacuzzi! At Aqua Velis in Mijas, Costa is one of the largest, splashiest water parks, with 21 rides to choose from. In Malaga, Costa del Sol is the Selwo Marine Park and the Benalmadena's Sea Life Centre. One can participate in an expedition to discover the sea life, birds, and ecosystems of the South American continent. It is the first interactive underwater park in Costa del Sol. You are allowed to walk across the bottom of the sea and gaze at almost 300,000 aquatic species.

Aqua Velis

Terra Metica

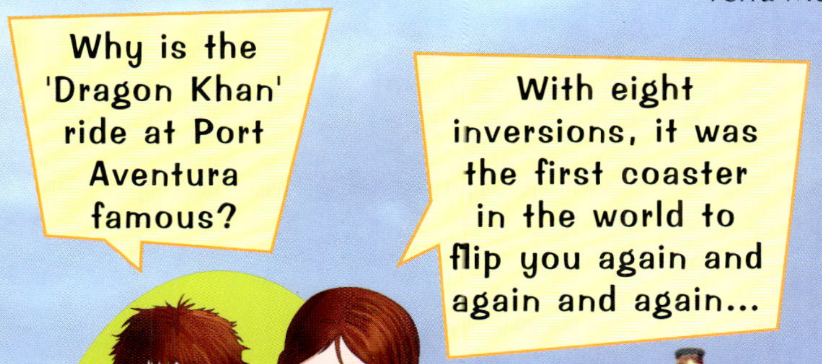

Base of Monte Igueldo

DID YOU KNOW?

- **Spanish inventor Manuel Jalon Corominas invented the mop in 1956. He designed it specially for women, who suffered pain and injuries in their hands and knees, while laboriously cleaning floors. The mop came to be called 'fregona' by his first salesman.**

Fregona

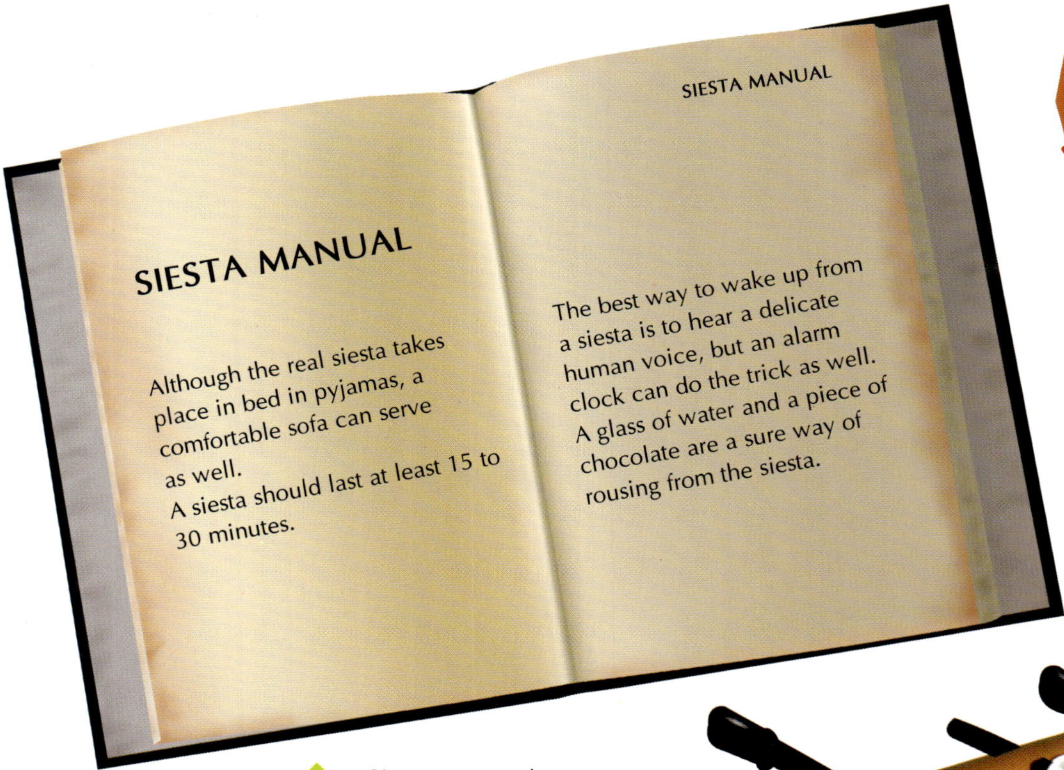

Siesta manual

- In order to fully enjoy a Spanish siesta or 'mañana' (an hour-long afternoon break from work, which also includes some zzzzzzzz), it is very important to have a good lunch with friends and/or relatives.

- Spain literally means ' the land of rabbits'.

- Hundreds of pet owners around Spain flock to the church on the day of San Anton to have their pets blessed by the patron saint of domestic animals.

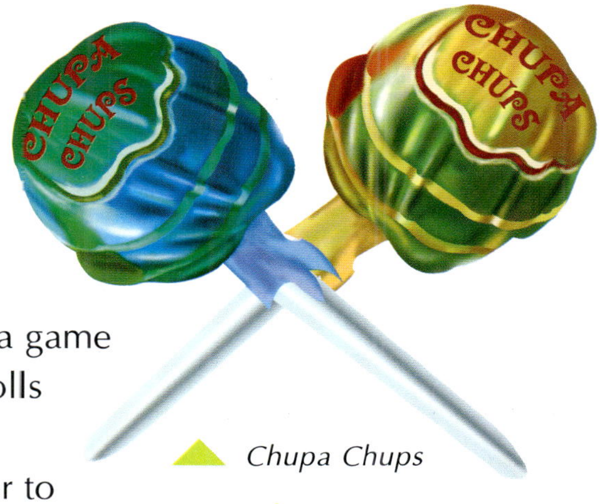

Chupa Chups

- Alexander Finisterre, a Galician poet, invented Futbolin, a game based on soccer. Futbolin is played on a table and has dolls mounted in rotating bars. The players have to move the bars to position their dolls, in order to hit the ball and score a goal. Today, it is popular all over the world.

- The Spanish lollipop is called Chupa Chups, which actually means 'round and long lasting'. Invented by Enric Bernat in 1958, the Chupa Chups logo was designed by Salvador Dali.

- The Episcopal Palace of King Philip II in the 16th century had 1200 doors!

- There are 21 Spanish-speaking countries in the world. The most difficult language is Basque as it is unrelated to any other language in the world.

Futbolin

- The name tarantula comes from a real spider that is found in Spain. It is not dangerous to humans! The people of Taranto believed that the only way to survive the bite of the spider was to do a dance called the 'Tarantella'. This involved very fast movements including jumping and the victim usually collapsed out of sheer exhaustion.

Tarantula

KNOW YOUR SPANISH

ENGLISH	SPANISH	PRONUNCIATION
How are you?	Cómo estás?	koh-moh ay-stahs
Hi! / Bye!	Hola! / Chao!	oh-lah / chow
Thank you	Gracias	(moo-chahs) grah-see-ahs
Yes / No	Sí / No	see / noh
My name is...	Me llamo...	may yah-moh
I'm from...	Yo soy de...	yoh soy day

Monday	lunes	loo-nays
Tuesday	martes	mar-tays
Wednesday	miércoles	mee-air-coh-lays
Thursday	jueves	hway-bays
Friday	viernes	bee-air-nays
Saturday	sábado	sah-bah-doh
Sunday	domingo	doh-ming-oh
the day	el día	ail dee-ah
the week	la semana	lah say-mahn-ah
the weekend	el fin de semana	ail feen day say-mahn-ah
today	hoy	oy
tomorrow	mañana	mahn-yahn-ah
my birthday	mi cumpleaños	mee coom-play-ahn-yohs

0	cero	cay-roh
1	uno	oo-noh
2	dos	dohs
3	tres	trays
4	cuatro	kuah-troh
5	cinco	seen-koh
6	seis	says
7	siete	see-ay-tay
8	ocho	oh-choh
9	nueve	new-ay-vay
10	diez	dee-ays